Snicker Rickers

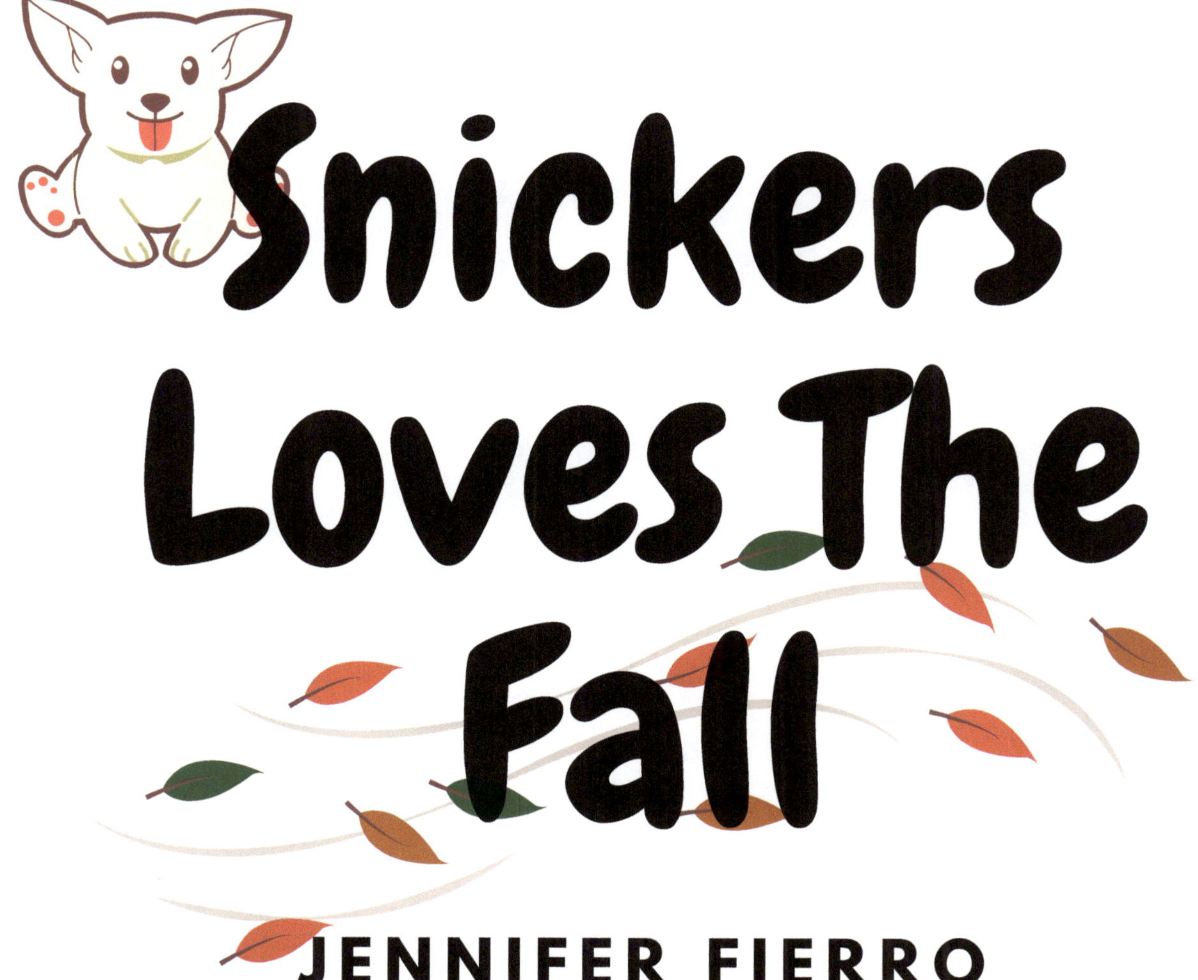

Snickers Loves The Fall

JENNIFER FIERRO

Dedications

TO MY DAUGHTER WHO HEARD COUNTLESS REVISIONS OF THIS SONNET. YOU'RE THE BEST.

I want to introduce you to Snickers.

Snickers loves taking walks around the house.  

She also loves hiding behind corners.

She loves not sleeping in her doghouse.

Even more
than that,
Snickers loves
the fall.

Yes, fall is Snickers' favorite season.

Snickers loves hearing the rain in the fall.

She smells yummy candles in the kitchen.

And the changing colors are fun to see.

Touching spooky pumpkins is also fun!

But so is feasting with her family.

Snickers loves sharing treats with everyone.

She loves to see, hear, taste, touch, smell it all.

Yes, without a doubt, Snickers loves the fall!

About the Author

JENNIFER HAS A DAUGHTER NAMED GENEVIEVE, WHO IS ALSO AN AUTHOR. JENNIFER HAS A DOGGIE AT HOME NAMED SNICKERS, WHO IS LOVINGLY REFERRED TO AS SNICKER RICKERS.